© **Copyright 2024 - All rights reserved.**

You may not reproduce, duplicate or send the contents of this book without direct written permission from the author. You cannot hereby despite any circumstance blame the publisher or hold him or her to legal responsibility for any reparation, compensations, or monetary forfeiture owing to the information included herein, either in a direct or an indirect way.

Legal Notice: This book has copyright protection. You can use the book for personal purposes. You should not sell, use, alter, distribute, quote, take excerpts, or paraphrase in part or whole the material contained in this book without obtaining the permission of the author first.

Disclaimer Notice: You must take note that the information in this document is for casual reading and entertainment purposes only. We have made every attempt to provide accurate, up-to-date, and reliable information. We do not express or imply guarantees of any kind. The persons who read admit that the writer is not occupied in giving legal, financial, medical, or other advice. We put this book content by sourcing various places.

Please consult a licensed professional before you try any techniques shown in this book. By going through this document, the book lover comes to an agreement that under no situation is the author accountable for any forfeiture, direct or indirect, which they may incur because of the use of material contained in this document, including, but not limited to, α errors, omissions, or inaccuracies.

Dieses Buch gehört ihm:

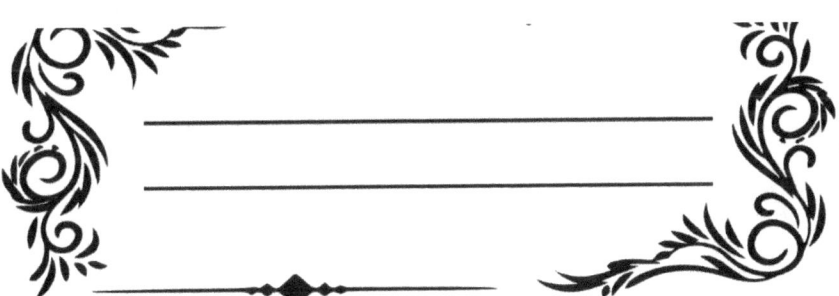

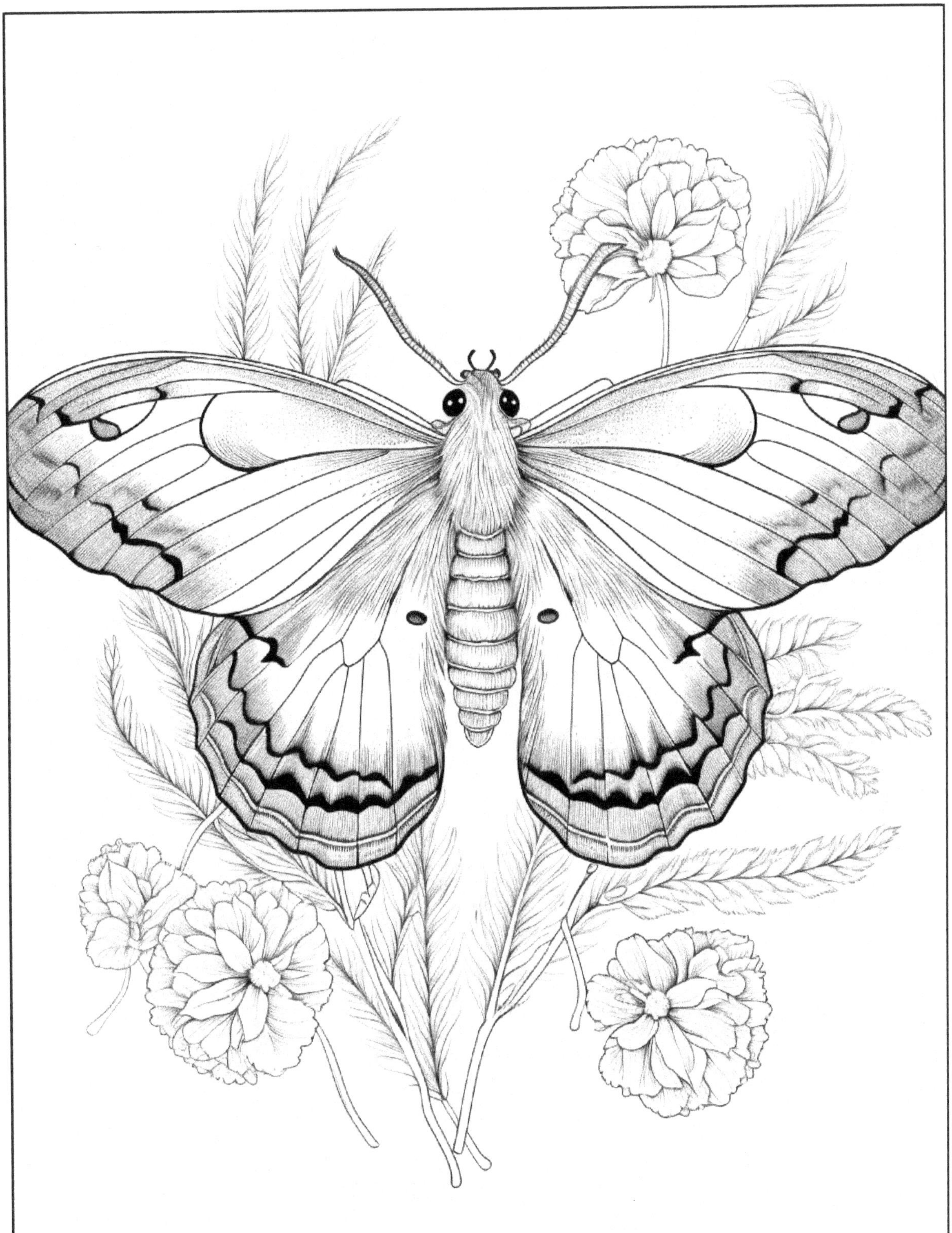

Thank You!

As the author of this gratitude journal, I wanted to take a moment to express our heartfelt gratitude for choosing our book and completing this incredible journey. It brings us great joy to know that our small, family-owned company has been a part of your life.

At our company, we pour our hearts and souls into creating quality children's books that inspire and empower young minds, just like you.

If you enjoyed this journal and found it to be a source of joy, encouragement, and growth, we kindly invite you to leave a review on Amazon. Your words carry immense power and can make a significant impact on our small business. Your support will not only help us reach more children but also inspire us to continue creating meaningful books.

We understand that leaving a review may seem like a small action, but to us, it means the world. Your support will enable us to continue producing quality books that touch the lives of young readers and nourish their imaginations.

This Is Our Family

Stela Stere

Cucus Surus

Tande Mande

 # Contact us!

It is important for us to let you know that we appreciate any feedback on our creations and if you have any suggestions for improvement, you can contact us at our email address:

gopublishforyou@gmail.com

Are you following us on Instagram?

If not, down below you can find the link to our Instagram page, where you can see other creations we have made, announcements about our books or announcements about our new releases.

https://www.instagram.com/cristiartdesign/